# Write On Girl!

## A fun guided journal for preteen girls

Written by Jillian D. Bradfield

Illustrated by Goldest Karat Art

# INTRODUCTION

## How do I use this thing?!

**Hey gorgeous girls!**
**This book is just for you!**

**Use this book to write your goals, dreams, and hearts desires. If you don't know where to begin, every week has topics to jumpstart your thoughts and get your creative juices flowing.**

**May you find joy and inspiration every week!**

NEW
YEAR
NEW
ME

# JANUARY

## New Year New Me!

**Write about your goals for the New Year. Ask yourself... Girl... What do I want to do differently this year? What sucked about last year?! What am I going to do to make it happen!?**

# JANUARY

## New Year New Me!

**Finish this thought:**
**If I could change one thing about myself ...**

**Be honest!**

# JANUARY

## New Year New Me!

**What's in a name? Research your name.**
**What does it mean?**
**Do you feel your name matches who you truly are?**

# JANUARY

## New Year New Me!

**Write 10 words that describe who you are.**
**Explain why you chose these particular words .**

# FEBRUARY

## Beautifully, Wonderfully Made Me!

**Activity: Create a Valentine's Day card for yourself!**
**For you, written by you.**
**All month long make it a point to speak positively about yourself.**

# FEBRUARY

## Beautifully, Wonderfully Made Me!

**You gotta love yourself first girl!**
**Valentine's Day is coming! Be your own Valentine!**
**Write about how much you love yourself, from your head to your toes!**

# FEBRUARY

## Beautifully, Wonderfully Made Me!

**What is self love to you and how do you show it?**

# FEBRUARY

## Beautifully, Wonderfully Made Me!

**Name someone that you absolutely, positively cannot stand! Then list reasons why? Do they make sense? Do you have some of the same characteristics as the person you don't like?**

# MARCH

## Random Thoughts

**Write about your favorite childhood memory so far.**

# MARCH

## Random Thoughts

**Write about the best or the worst day of your life. Why was it so bad?**

# MARCH

## Random Thoughts

**Do you have a male role model in your life?**
**Who is it and why? What have they taught you?**

# MARCH

## Random Thoughts

**If you could give yourself any super power, what would it be?**

# APRIL

## Decisions, Decisions

**If you have a friend that told you they drink alcohol or did drugs, how would you help them? What would you do if they offered the drugs or alcohol to you?**

# APRIL

## Decisions, Decisions

**If you had a million dollars, how would you spend it?**

# APRIL

## Decisions, Decisions

**When was the last time you told a lie? Why?
What was the lie and did it affect you in the long run?**

# APRIL

## Decisions, Decisions

**Think about a time you had to make a very hard decision between right and wrong. What did you decide to do? How do you feel about the decision now?**

# MAY

My future is so bright I need shades on!

**Five years from now, I will be...**

# MAY

## My future is so bright I need shades on!

**My ideal career is...**

# MAY

## My future is so bright I need shades on!

**Activity: Research this career and make your own career plan! What steps will you have to take to get there?**

# MAY

My future is so bright I need shades on!

**What is a secret talent that you have that no one knows about?!**

# JUNE

## Not So Different After All

**Write about a person that you know with special needs. Who are they? Do you talk to them?**

# JUNE

## Not So Different After All

**Have you ever made fun of someone that looked different than you? How did that make you feel? What was different about them?**

# JUNE

## Not So Different After All

**What would you do if your friends start to make fun of or laugh at someone that has a disability?**

# JUNE

## Not So Different After All

**Activity: Make a new friend! Sit next to someone that you usually wouldn't sit next to at lunch. Start a conversation with them. You may learn you two have a lot in common.**

# JULY

Summertime! It's hot outside and school is out!

**When is the last time you've done something nice for someone ? What did you do?**

# JULY

Summertime! It's hot outside and school is out!

**Activity: Help your parent by offering to do a chore without being told. What was their response?**

# JULY

## Summertime! It's hot outside and school is out!

**Activity: My grandma always said, " An idle mind is the devil's playground!" Don't be idle this summer! Research volunteer opportunities in your community and sign up for them. Volunteering is a great way to put your extra time to great use.**

# JULY

Summertime! It's hot outside and school is out!

**What volunteer activity did you decide to participate in? Who did you meet? Will you do it again?**

# JULY

Summertime! It's hot outside and school is out!

**Take this time to thank your loved ones for different things. I mean really think about it. Name different people that you are thankful for and write them a thank you note below.**

SLAY GIRL!

# AUGUST

Love your skin. Love its flaws. Embrace your body and all its uniqueness! ~Jillian

**Activity: Take magazine clippings and make a collage of pictures and words you feel represent beauty!**

# AUGUST

Love your skin. Love its flaws. Embrace your body and all its uniqueness! ~Jillian

**What is beautiful to you? Do you think you're beautiful?**

# AUGUST

Love your skin. Love its flaws. Embrace your body and all its uniqueness! ~Jillian

**Write about the last time you received a compliment. What was it? Who said it?**

# AUGUST

Love your skin. Love its flaws. Embrace your body and all its uniqueness! ~Jillian

**When do you feel beautiful or pretty? Is there a difference?**

YOU'RE CUTE

# SEPTEMBER

## Let's Talk About Sex !!

**Sex is a tricky subject. You think you know but you have no idea! Not only does sex include physical contact but it includes your feelings, health, and your heart! Know that you're worth waiting for pretty girl! Your body is your own and the only one you get, so take care of it!!**

# SEPTEMBER

## Let's Talk About Sex! !

**Soooo who is he?! Name the person you have a crush on and why?**

# SEPTEMBER

## Let's Talk About Sex!!

**Have they asked you to have sex? What did you say? Why? (you better say no ☺ )**

# SEPTEMBER

## Let's Talk About Sex!!

**What do you know about your crush?!**

# SEPTEMBER

## Let's Talk About Sex! !

**Books before babies: Make a list of what could happen if you have sex.**

**Hint: You can get more than just babies! But think seriously about this list.**

# SEPTEMBER

## Let's Talk About Sex! !

**Bonus Writing Activity:**
**Do you feel that you're ready for such a big decision?**

**Another Hint: You are not. ☺ But write out your thoughts.**

# OCTOBER

This won't last long sweety!

Pain is only temporary.

**We are always stronger once we get through it!**
**Don't make a permanent decision because of a temporary feeling or situation.**

**When is the last time you felt pain? Who hurt you?**

# OCTOBER

This won't last long sweety !
Pain is only temporary.

**Complete this sentence: When I am sad I ...**

# OCTOBER

This won't last long sweety !

Pain is only temporary.

**Write about a time when you were so depressed you didn't want to be here anymore. Did you tell someone about it?**

# OCTOBER

This won't last long sweety!
Pain is only temporary.

**Talk to your close friends. Ask them if they are ok. Are they having issues at home? Ask 5 people how they have been feeling and just be a listening ear. What did you learn?**

That's a nice shirt even though it's a knock off
You smell that? It didn't stink until she got over here
TREE OF SHADE
NOT NAME BRAND

# NOVEMBER

## Don't mind me, I'm just sitting under this shade tree...

**For the entire month of November I dare you not to throw shade! See how good it feels to express yourself directly with your words. Thou Shalt Not Shade ~ Jillian**

**What is shade to you? Are you a shady individual?**

# NOVEMBER

Don't mind me, I'm just sitting under this shade tree...

**When is the last time you threw shade? Why? Did it make you feel important? Smart? Better? What did you say?**

# NOVEMBER

Don't mind me, I'm just sitting under this shade tree...

**Who are your enemies? Why? Do they even know you don't like them? Do you know why you don't like them?**

# NOVEMBER

Don't mind me, I'm just sitting under this shade tree...

**Activity: How do you shade thee? Let me count the shade~**

**Watch some of your favorite shows! But you must count the times then explain in detail when you detect shade.**

END
OF
THE
ROAD

# DECEMBER

## Year End Wrap Up!

**Tell me what you learned about yourself this year.**

# DECEMBER

## Year End Wrap Up!

**How do you feel about this time of year? Why?**

# DECEMBER

## Year End Wrap Up!

**Did you lose any friends this year? Make some new ones? If so, who is no longer in your circle of friends and why? Who are the new friends and why?**

# DECEMBER

## Year End Wrap Up!

**As the year comes to a close, reflect and think about your life. Did you accomplish your goals? How did you grow? Tell me about it girl!**

Made in the USA
Middletown, DE
11 October 2023